Amazing Inventions

Inventing Drones

by Donna B. McKinney

www.focusreaders.com

Focus Readers is distributed by North Star Editions:
sales@northstareditions.com | 888-417-0195

Produced for Focus Readers by Red Line Editorial.

Photographs ©: Shutterstock Images, cover, 1, 4, 7, 11, 13, 14, 17, 18, 20–21, 22, 25, 27, 29; clu/DigitalVision Vectors/Getty Images, 8

Library of Congress Cataloging-in-Publication Data
Names: McKinney, Donna Bowen, author.
Title: Inventing drones / by Donna B. McKinney.
Description: Lake Elmo, MN : Focus Readers, [2022] | Series: Amazing inventions | Includes index. | Audience: Grades 2-3
Identifiers: LCCN 2021041733 (print) | LCCN 2021041734 (ebook) | ISBN 9781637390467 (hardcover) | ISBN 9781637391006 (paperback) | ISBN 9781637391549 (ebook) | ISBN 9781637392058 (pdf)
Subjects: LCSH: Drone aircraft--Juvenile literature.
Classification: LCC TL685.35 .M38 2022 (print) | LCC TL685.35 (ebook) | DDC 629.133/39--dc23
LC record available at https://lccn.loc.gov/2021041733
LC ebook record available at https://lccn.loc.gov/2021041734

Printed in the United States of America
Mankato, MN
012022

About the Author

Donna B. McKinney has an MA in English from George Mason University. She spent many years writing about science and technology at the US Naval Research Laboratory in Washington, DC. Now she enjoys writing about topics ranging from science to history to sports for children and young adults.

Table of Contents

Chapter 1

A View from Above

One night, a tornado hits a town. Its strong wind flips cars and smashes windows. By the morning, many buildings have been damaged. One home's roof is completely torn off.

 Drones can help workers search for survivors after earthquakes or storms.

A tiny aircraft flies above the damage. There is no pilot inside it. That's because it's a drone. A person on the ground controls it. He uses a remote control. He steers the drone. He uses its camera to take pictures from the air.

Soon after, rescue workers arrive. The drone's pictures show them

Did You Know?

Drones are also called "unmanned aerial vehicles," or UAVs.

 Many drones can send photos and information to computers, tablets, and smartphones.

where to go. They help clean up.

And they check for people who have

been hurt.

Chapter 2

Drone History

Drones are aircraft with no pilots. **Militaries** made the first drones. In the 1800s, some armies used hot-air balloons. The balloons flew over enemy land and dropped bombs. They were hard to steer.

Long ago, some armies used hot-air balloons to spy on enemies.

Wind often blew them off course. Soldiers wanted more control. So, they invented UAVs.

The first UAVs were used during World War I (1914–1918). They looked like small airplanes. But they had no pilots. Instead, people steered them from the ground. They

Did You Know?

In 1935, the British army made a UAV called the Queen Bee. After that, people began calling UAVs *drones*. A drone is a male bee.

 The V-1 was a flying bomb used by Germany during World War II (1939–1945).

used radio signals. The signals traveled through the air. They told the UAVs where to go. Some of these early drones were weapons.

Others were targets for people to shoot.

In the Vietnam War (1954–1975), soldiers began using drones for spying. They put cameras on drones. The drones took pictures. The pictures showed what enemies were doing. Using these drones was safer than having pilots fly over enemy areas.

People continued making new kinds of drones. Over time, drones began to cost less to build. As a

 US laws first let people fly drones for businesses in 2006.

result, more people could buy them. Laws about drones changed as well. At first, only militaries could use drones. Later, **civilians** were allowed to use drones, too. Today, many people fly drones for fun.

Chapter 3

Parts of a Drone

Drones come in many shapes and sizes. However, there are a few main types of drones. One type looks like a small helicopter. It has one **rotor**. Other types of drones use multiple rotors to fly and turn.

 Fixed-wing drones are designed to fly long distances.

A fixed-wing drone looks more like an airplane. Instead of rotors, it has wings and **propellers**.

All drones have a power source. Some drones have batteries. Others use fuel. Each drone also has a computer. It controls the drone. However, people must give it instructions. They often use

Did You Know?

Rotor drones can hover in one spot in the air. Fixed-wing drones cannot.

Different Drones

Multirotor drones and fixed-wing drones are two of the most popular types.

Multirotor Drones

- can fly straight up and down
- tend to be more stable
- can be steered more precisely
- can carry more weight

Fixed-Wing Drones

- can fly faster and higher
- can make longer flights
- are easier to repair
- fly better during weather

controllers to do this. A controller sends signals to the drone. These signals tell the drone how to move. Some drones can be **programmed**.

A screen on the controller shows what the drone's camera sees.

People write a set of instructions for the drone's computer. They explain each step it needs to do. Some drones have other parts, too. Many drones use **GPS**. It helps them not get lost. Other tools help a drone measure speed or **altitude**. A drone may also have sensors. They may check the temperature. Or they may test the air for chemicals. Many drones carry cameras. They take pictures or videos from the air.

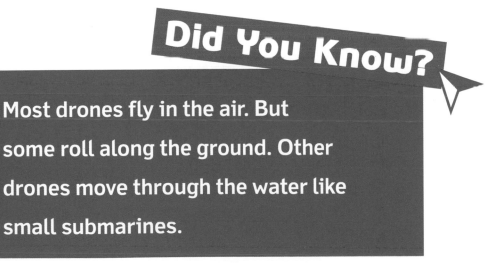

Did You Know?

Most drones fly in the air. But some roll along the ground. Other drones move through the water like small submarines.

Controlling a Drone

A multirotor drone has several rotors. They spin like fans. Each rotor pushes air down as it spins. The air pushes back against the rotor. It creates a force called lift. This force moves the drone up into the air.

People control how the drone flies by changing the rotors' speeds. When rotors spin faster, they create more lift. As a result, the drone flies higher. To get the drone to fly lower, people slow the rotors. Changing the speed of the rotors on just one side makes the drone **tilt** or turn.

A quadcopter is a type of drone with four rotors.

Chapter 4

What Drones Do

Today, people use drones in many ways. Some drones deliver packages. Other drones collect information. Drones help map land and track storms. They can help search for missing people.

 Many drones fly near power lines or power plants. They help check for problems.

Filmmakers even use drones to make movies.

Militaries continue to use drones as well. They keep making newer and better versions. Some of these drones are very tiny. Soldiers use them to spy on enemies. The drones are hard to see. Drones also help

Did You Know?

Some drones bring medical supplies to **remote** areas. They help save people's lives.

Military drones often fly over enemy lands.

with fighting. They may shoot or carry weapons.

Drones are often used for risky or difficult jobs. For example, drones can fly to dangerous places. People control the drones from far away.

If something goes wrong, the people won't get hurt.

However, drones have some downsides. Many make noise as they fly. They can also get in the way of airplanes. For these reasons, laws prevent drones from flying at certain times or places. Even so,

Did You Know?

Scientists use drones to study penguins in Antarctica. They fly groups of drones that take pictures.

 Many drones must stay below 400 feet (122 m). This rule helps them avoid aircraft.

people keep thinking of new uses

for drones. For example, some

drones help farmers care for plants.

FOCUS ON
Inventing Drones

Write your answers on a separate piece of paper.

1. Write a sentence describing one task that drones help people do.

2. Do you think it would be fun to own a drone? Why or why not?

3. When were the first UAVs used?
   - **A.** in the 1800s
   - **B.** in World War I
   - **C.** in the 1960s

4. Why would lowering the rotor speed make a drone fly lower?
   - **A.** Lower speed would create less force.
   - **B.** Lower speed would create more force.
   - **C.** Lower speed would create no force at all.

5. What does **hover** mean in this book?

*Rotor drones can **hover** in one spot in the air.*

    A. to swing far to the left

    B. to stay in one place in the air

    C. to land on the ground

6. What does **pilot** mean in this book?

*A tiny aircraft flies above the damage. There is no **pilot** inside it.*

    A. a person who flies an aircraft

    B. a person who sinks a boat

    C. a person who cooks food

Answer key on page 32.

Glossary

altitude
Height above the ground.

civilians
People who are not in the military.

GPS
Short for "global positioning system," a navigation system that uses satellites to figure out location.

militaries
Groups of soldiers or armed forces.

programmed
When a machine is given a set of instructions so that it can perform an action.

propellers
Vertical sets of spinning blades that provide thrust, which moves a vehicle forward.

remote
Far away from cities or other places.

rotor
A horizontal set of spinning blades that provide lift, which moves a vehicle up into the air.

tilt
To lean or tip in one direction.

To Learn More

BOOKS

Faust, Daniel R. *How Do Drones Work?* New York: PowerKids Press, 2021.

Lanier, Wendy Hinote. *Drones*. Lake Elmo, MN: Focus Readers, 2019.

Olson, Elsie. *Drones*. Minneapolis: Abdo Publishing, 2018.

NOTE TO EDUCATORS

Visit **www.focusreaders.com** to find lesson plans, activities, links, and other resources related to this title.

Index